Moroccan Foods & Culture

by Jennifer Ferro

The Rourke Press, Inc.
Vero Beach, FL 32964

Note to Readers: The recipes in this book are meant to be enjoyed by young people. Children should ask an adult for help, however, when preparing any recipe involving knives, blenders, or other sharp implements and the use of stoves, microwaves, or other heating appliances.

On the Cover: *A Moroccan man pours mint tea in a traditional ceremony.*

Photo Credits: Cover photo Omni-Photo/Esbin/Anderson; p. 4 EyeWire; p. 6 CORBIS/ Gary Aurness; p. 9 Len Kaufman; p. 10 CORBIS/Owen Franken; p. 12, 32 PhotoDisc; p. 13, 23 CORBIS/Michelle Garrett; p. 14 Publishers Depot; p. 19, 30, 41 Paul O'Connor; p. 22 CORBIS/Penny Tweedie; p. 33 William B. Folsom.

Produced by Salem Press, Inc.

Library of Congress Cataloging-in-Publication Data

Ferro, Jennifer. 1968-
    Moroccan foods and culture / Jennifer Ferro.
    p.   cm. — (Festive foods & celebrations)
    Summary: Discusses some of the foods enjoyed in Morocco and describes special foods that are part of such specific celebrations as Ramadan, the Great Festival for Abraham, and weddings. Includes recipes.
    ISBN 1-57103-304-1
    1. Cookery, Moroccan Juvenile literature. 2. Food habits—Morocco Juvenile literature. 3. Festivals—Morocco Juvenile literature. [1. Food habits—Morocco. 2. Cookery, Moroccan. 3. Festivals—Morocco. 4. Holidays—Morocco. 5. Morocco—Social life and customs.] I. Title. II. Series: Ferro, Jennifer. 1968-   Festive foods & celebrations.
TX725.M8F47   1999
641.5964—dc21   99-21049
                                                                                  CIP

First Printing

Contents

Introduction to Morocco

Morocco (muh-RAW-koh) is a country on the northern coast of the *continent* (KON-tun-unt) of *Africa* (AH-frih-kuh). It *borders* the *Mediterranean Sea* (meh-duh-tuh-RAY-nee-un see) and the Atlantic Ocean. Three hours from the sea are the Atlas Mountains. They are covered with snow. People who live in Morocco are called Moroccans (muh-RAW-kunz).

Morocco has a very old *culture* (KULL-chur). The Berber (BUR-bur) people have lived there for

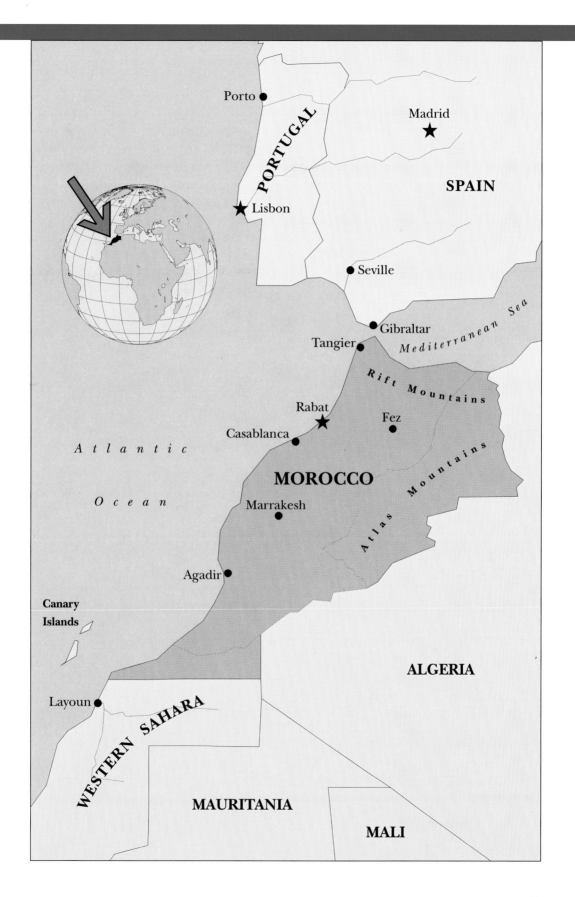

Porto

PORTUGAL

Madrid

SPAIN

Lisbon

Seville

Gibraltar

Tangier

Mediterranean Sea

Rift Mountains

Rabat

Fez

Casablanca

MOROCCO

Atlas Mountains

Atlantic

Ocean

Marrakesh

Agadir

Canary
Islands

ALGERIA

Layoun

WESTERN SAHARA

MAURITANIA

MALI

A nomad leads his camels across the desert.

thousands of years. Most Berbers are nomads
(NOH-madz). This means they do not have
permanent homes. These Berber families follow
sheep and other animals that walk the land to
graze. Moroccan culture has also been influenced
by Arabs. Arabic (AIR-uh-bick) is the official
language of Morocco.

In 1492, many people left Spain to live in
Morocco. These Spanish people brought many
foods with them. One food was a dough as thin as

paper. They also brought couscous (KOOS-koos). You will learn how to make this dish later in the book. Morocco was ruled by France from 1912 to 1956. Many Moroccans still speak the French language.

The religion of most people in Morocco is Islam (iz-LOM). Islam was founded in the 7th century by *Muhammad* (moh-HOM-ud). He was a prophet or holy man. People who practice Islam are called Muslims (MUZ-lumz). The holy books in Islam are the *Bible* and a book of Muhammad's teachings called the Koran or *Qur'an* (kuh-RON).

In some ways, Morocco has not changed in hundreds of years. People ride camels and donkeys in the countryside. Men and women wear robes with hoods like people did long ago.

In the countryside, water does not come out of a faucet. Women walk to a well to get fresh water. They take empty jugs to the well and fill them. They carry the jugs of water on their heads as they walk home.

One of the main cities in Morocco is Marrakesh (MARE-uh-kesh). On its streets you can see snake charmers, sword swallowers, vegetable sellers, and *acrobats*.

Shoppers go to outdoor markets called souks (SOOKZ) to buy *spices*. Spices are very important to Moroccan cooking. Each spice seller has his own secret blend. Spices like *cumin* (KYOO-mun) and cinnamon are often used.

Moroccans also use saffron (SAH-frun) in their cooking. Saffron is the most expensive spice in the world. A *pinch* of it has enough flavor for a whole meal. It takes 75,000 blossoms of a special flower to make 1 pound of this spice. All the blossoms have to be picked by hand.

People in Morocco eat at large round tables that are low to the ground. They sit on cushions with their legs crossed. Moroccans are generous people. They always make space at their tables for new guests.

Food is served in large dishes, usually in mounds. Moroccans do not eat with forks and knives. They

Mounds of colorful spices are sold in a Moroccan market.

use the thumb and first two fingers of the right hand instead. The left hand is never used. People take small handfuls of food and roll them into balls. They push the food into their mouths with

A boy sells olives in a store in Marrakesh.

their first two fingers. Moroccans also use bread as a spoon to grab food. They dip the bread into sauces and into the mounds of food.

Over a million fruit trees grow in Morocco—oranges, lemons, figs, dates, and almonds. Olive trees also grow there. Every December, men *harvest* the olives from the trees. They hit the trunks with heavy sticks to make the olives fall off.

The olives are gathered and pressed to make *olive oil*. This oil is used for cooking. Olives are also *cured* and eaten whole. Many different types of olives are eaten in Morocco. People eat olives flavored with lemon and garlic or with hot red chilis.

Weddings

In Morocco, people who get married do not always fall in love first. Often their parents decide that they would make a good match. Sometimes, the bride and groom have never met before the wedding.

A wedding in Morocco is a big feast with many ceremonies. It lasts seven days. For most of these days, the bride and groom do not see each other. The bride has parties each night with only women. The groom has parties each night with only men.

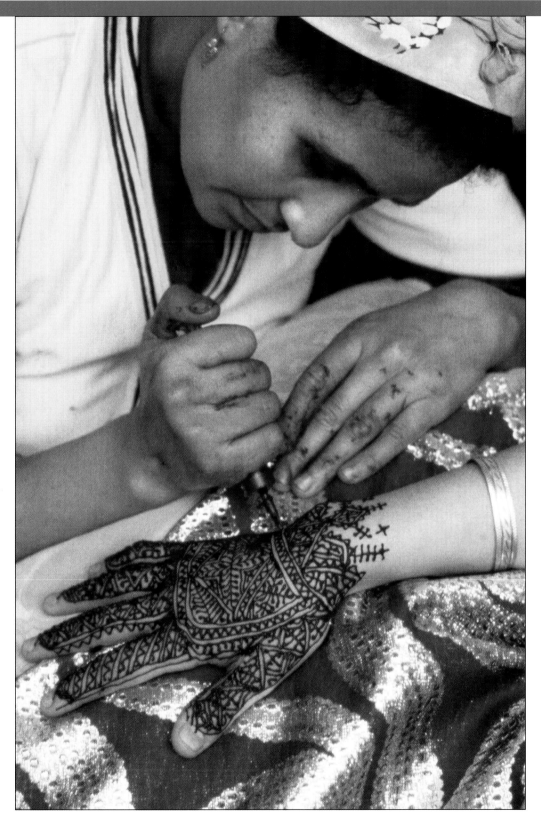

A woman draws designs on the bride's hands using henna.

This Moroccan bride wears a lot of jewelry and colorful robes to her wedding.

Every night, the friends and sisters of the bride lead her to a special bath. They wash her and stay with her until morning. People play drums and sing when the bride walks back to the wedding ceremony each morning.

On the seventh day, the bride is dressed in green and white. She is now ready for the henna ceremony. Henna is a reddish dye. A special artist draws designs on the bride's feet and hands. This takes many hours. The designs look like *tattoos*. The dye comes off in a few days.

The bride's hair is washed with henna. The dye is left on her hair to dry in the sun. Then her hair is washed out and scented with roses and cinnamon. The bride's hair is styled with bright ribbons and combs.

The bride's face is decorated with makeup and jewels. She will change clothes and jewelry seven different times during the day. Each new costume represents a different region of Morocco.

The groom is also taken to a bath. Then he goes

Dates

Dates are sweet fruits used in Moroccan cooking and ceremonies. The word "date" comes from the Greek word for "finger" because dates look like fingers. Dates grow on date palm trees. The date palm tree is known as the Tree of Life because it is mentioned in the Bible. These trees can grow to 100 feet tall and have over 1,000 dates on them. The fruit grows in bunches of 200 dates that can weigh 40 pounds. Dates are used in all kinds of cereals and in fig cookies.

to the center of the town. He waits for the bride's family to meet him and bring him back to the wedding. The groom is led to the bride. He is followed by musicians and singers.

This is the first time that the groom kisses the bride. He kisses her on the forehead. The groom gives the bride a date to eat and milk to drink. She hands him a date and some milk too.

All the guests drink hot mint tea. They eat little cakes made of almonds and honey.

The bride and groom sit in the middle of the room together as the guests eat and dance. Finally, at midnight everyone sits down to enjoy the huge feast.

First, each guest's hands are washed. A handful of warm water is poured in their hands. They dry their hands and receive a few drops of orange-flower water, a liquid scented with oranges.

Many different plates of food are placed in the center of round tables. Desserts are passed around. When everyone is finished eating, the married couple is carried on the shoulders of the guests. Then they are left alone together.

Spiced Meatballs

1 small onion

1 pound of ground beef

1 egg

1/2 cup of dried bread crumbs

1 teaspoon of allspice

2 teaspoons of salt

black pepper

2 cups of spaghetti sauce

- Cut the onion in half. Peel off the skin and some outer layers. Rub against the large holes of a grater.

- Break the egg into a bowl. Beat it lightly with a fork.

- Place the ground beef into a large bowl. Add the onion, bread crumbs, egg, allspice, salt, and some black pepper.

Mix with your hands. Wait 10 minutes. Form small handfuls of the mixture into balls or flatten into patties.

◆ Heat the spaghetti sauce in a pan on medium-low. Add the meatballs. Cover

Spiced Meatballs with Hummus and Pita Bread

and cook for 10 to 12 minutes. Make sure they cook all the way through.

◆ Serve with or without the sauce. The meatballs can be served around a cup of rice with cinnamon sprinkled on top. They can also be served with hummus and pita bread. Serves 6.

Moroccan Orange Salad

6 oranges
12 dates
1/4 cup of slivered almonds
orange-flower water or lemon juice
powdered cinnamon

◆ Peel the oranges. Try to use navel oranges because they are seedless.

Remove the rind. Slice the oranges into circles and then into strips.

◆ Squeeze the pits out of the dates. Chop the dates into small chunks.

◆ Put the dates and oranges into a bowl. Sprinkle slivered almonds on top. Drizzle a few drops of orange-flower water or lemon juice into the bowl.

◆ Cover with plastic wrap and refrigerate. Sprinkle powdered cinnamon on top just before serving.

Ramadan

Ramadan (raw-muh-DON) is a religious holiday. It is a very important time for Muslims. Ramadan lasts for 30 days.

Muslims believe that eating and drinking stops you from thinking about God. Not eating or drinking is called having a *fast*. Muslims believe that fasting cleans out the body and cleans out thoughts in the mind.

During the month of Ramadan, Muslims are not allowed to eat or drink from sunrise to sunset.

A traditional dinner to break the Ramadan fast consists of soup, hard-boiled eggs, and dates.

Nothing can pass their lips while the sun is up. That way, they can focus on their religion.

Every morning during Ramadan, Muslims wake up before sunrise. They eat a large breakfast with their family. Muslims are allowed to eat again only when they cannot tell the difference outside between a white thread and a black thread. Only then is it considered dark.

Muslims believe that Muhammad ate dates when

Mint Tea

The national drink in Morocco is mint tea. It is made using Chinese green tea leaves. Traders from England brought Chinese tea around 1850. Moroccans added fresh mint leaves and lots of sugar. Moroccans drink tea in the middle of the morning and after each meal. Tea drinking takes time and can never be hurried. When the tea is ready, one glass is poured out and poured back into the teapot. Then the tea is served in small decorated glasses. The person who is pouring holds the teapot high in the air and lets the tea fall into the glasses. Guests must drink at least three glasses to show their thanks.

he broke his fast over a thousand years ago. That is why they eat dates to break their fast every night after sunset. Dates are very sweet. They turn into a brown sugar after they are picked. Dates are sometimes called "nature's candy."

Each night, Muslims in Morocco also eat a *hard-boiled* egg, a special bread, and a bowl of Ramadan soup. This soup is very nutritious (new-TRIH-shuss). It is a good food to eat after a whole day of fasting.

Ramadan is a time for helping the poor and being kind to friends, family, and strangers. Being unkind or eating something during the day breaks the fast. The 30 days of fasting have to start all over again.

At the end of Ramadan, Muslims celebrate with a big party and a feast. They invite neighbors, family, and friends to share in the meal. They dress in their nicest clothes and jewelry. Children get toys, money, and sweets.

Ramadan Soup

1 onion

2 boneless chicken breasts

8 cups of water

1/4 cup of canned lentils, pinto beans, or black-eyed peas

1/2 cup of rice

1 cup of stewed tomatoes

1/2 cup of fresh chopped parsley or 1/4 cup of dried parsley

2 cups of canned chickpeas (garbanzo beans)

1 egg

1/4 cup of lemon juice

salt and pepper

1 package of pita bread

♦ Chop the onion into pieces. Cut the chicken breasts into chunks.

- Put the onion, chicken, and water into a large saucepan. Bring to a boil on high heat. Stir. Turn the heat down to *simmer*. Cover and cook for 25 minutes.

- Stir in the lentils, rice, stewed tomatoes (with juice), and parsley. Bring to a boil on high heat. Turn the heat down to simmer. Cover and cook for another 20 minutes.

- Add the chickpeas (with juice).

- Crack the egg into a bowl. Beat it lightly with a fork. Stir while you add the beaten egg.

- Add the lemon juice and a little salt and pepper. Simmer with the lid off for 10 minutes.

◆ Pour into bowls. Serve with *pita bread*. Serves 6.

Date Bars

10 ounces of dates (pitted, dried, and chopped)
2/3 cup of water
2/3 cup of sugar
1/3 cup of fresh lemon juice
1 package of premade pie crusts

◆ Preheat the oven to 425 degrees.

◆ Put the dates and water into a saucepan over medium-high heat. Bring the water to a boil. Turn the heat down to medium. Cook for 5 minutes, until it looks thick.

- Stir in the sugar. Remove the pan from the stove. Add the lemon juice. Set aside to cool.

- Spray a 9 x 9 glass or metal baking pan with nonstick cooking spray.

- Lay out one pie crust in the baking pan. Cut off the extra crust so it lays flat. Pour the date mixture on top.

- Lay the second crust on top of the date mixture. Cut off the extra crust so it lays flat. Slit the top of the crust with a knife.

- Bake for 35 to 40 minutes, until the crust is golden brown.

- Let cool and then cut into bars. Makes 9 bars.

Mint Tea

5 cups of water

2 tea bags of Chinese green tea

1/2 cup of sugar

15 fresh mint leaves

1 cinnamon stick

Mint Tea with Dates and Almonds

- Boil the water in a teakettle.

- Place the tea bags into a teapot or pitcher. Pour the boiling water over the tea bags. Let the tea *steep* for 2 minutes.

- Add the sugar, mint leaves, and cinnamon stick. Let the tea steep for 4 more minutes.

- Pour the tea into small glasses or teacups. Makes 5 cups.

The Great Festival

The Great Festival is held 50 days after the end of Ramadan. It also called the Feast of the Lamb. The Great Festival celebrates the story of Abraham and Isaac in the Bible. God told Abraham to kill his only son Isaac. This was a test. Abraham could prove his love for God if he would do whatever God asked.

Abraham took Isaac to a mountain to *sacrifice* him. God stopped him before he could kill his son. He rewarded Abraham for his loyalty. God

During the Great Festival, lamb is served to remember Abraham's sacrifice.

Couscous

Couscous is the national dish of Morocco. It is served at the end of a large meal in a big mound like a mountain. Moroccans have been eating couscous since the 13th century. Couscous is made from wheat flour formed into tiny grains. It is said that each grain stands for a good deed. Cooks hide small pieces of meat in the couscous to ensure good luck. They decorate the "face" of the mound with vegetables, meat, or fish. The couscous is put in the center of the table. People grab small handfuls with their fingers, roll them into balls, and push them into their mouths.

promised that Abraham would have as many *descendants* (dih-SEN-duntz) as there are grains of sand on the seashore. A lamb appeared. Abraham killed it for God instead.

In Morocco, every family kills a sheep or lamb during the Great Festival to honor Abraham.

Families that do not have a lamb will buy one a month earlier to fatten it up.

Each family kills a lamb at 11:00 o'clock on the morning of the Great Festival. Then everyone prays. Muslims believe that all the prayers of all the Muslims around the world come together at this moment.

The festival lasts four days. Many dishes made with lamb are eaten to celebrate. Every part of the lamb is eaten. Nothing is wasted. Sons and daughters who live away from home come back to celebrate with their families. Friends and family are invited to share in the great feast.

On the first day, people eat lamb *kebabs* (kuh-BOBZ). Kebabs are *cubes* of lamb put on a stick and roasted over a fire. Lamb couscous and lamb stew are also served during the Great Festival.

The Berber people have a special lamb dish that is served on this day. Berbers roast a whole lamb over a large firepit in the ground. The lamb is brushed with butter and salt and turned slowly over the fire. It takes up to 4 hours to cook. Then the lamb is ready to be eaten by a large group of people. Guests take a piece of lamb and a handful of couscous.

Lamb Kebabs

2 pounds of boneless lamb shank

1 onion

1 red pepper

1 green pepper

6 metal or wood skewers

salt and pepper

♦ Preheat the oven to 400 degrees.

♦ Cut the lamb into 3-inch cubes. Cut the onion into 6 large pieces.

♦ Cut open the red and green peppers. Throw out the seeds. Chop them into 6 large pieces each.

♦ Poke a lamb cube with a skewer. Slide it to near the bottom. Poke a piece of onion with the same skewer. Slide it on top of the lamb. Poke a piece of pepper. Slide it on top of the onion. Repeat until the skewer is full.

- Repeat until all the skewers are full.

- Spray a 13 x 9 cake pan with nonstick cooking spray. Lay the skewers in the pan. Sprinkle with some salt and pepper. Wrap the pan with foil so the skewers are covered.

- Bake for 20 minutes, until the meat and onions are tender when pierced with a fork. Serves 6.

Glazed Carrots

2 pounds of carrots

salt

4 tablespoons of olive oil

2 tablespoons of sugar

2 tablespoons of lemon juice

2 tablespoons or half a bunch of
   cilantro

hot red pepper flakes

◆ Peel the carrots. Cut them into
   pieces about the size of a quarter.

◆ Cut the stems off the cilantro.
   Throw them away. Chop the leaves
   into small pieces.

◆ Fill a saucepan 1/2 full with water.
   Boil the water on high heat. Add a
   bit of salt.

- ◆ Add the carrots. Cook for 12 minutes, until they are tender. Drain.

- ◆ Add the olive oil, sugar, lemon juice, and cilantro. Stir.

- ◆ Sprinkle on a few hot red pepper flakes. (Be careful! They are very hot.) Serves 4.

Couscous

1 box of couscous
10 carrots
3 zucchini or Italian squash
1 bunch of cilantro

- ◆ Peel the carrots. Cut them into small pieces.

- Slice the tips off the zucchini. Chop the zucchini into small pieces.

- Cut the stems off the cilantro. Throw them away. Chop the leaves into small pieces.

Couscous with Pita Bread, Dates, and Almonds

- Prepare the couscous according to the directions on the package.

- Spoon the couscous into a large serving bowl.

- Add the zucchini, carrots, and cilantro. Stir. Serves 4.

Glossary

acrobat: a person who can flip his or her body forward and backward.

Africa: a large continent with such countries as Morocco, Sudan, South Africa, and Egypt.

Bible: a holy book that Christians, Jews, and Muslims believe tells the story of God.

boil: to heat water or another liquid until it starts to bubble.

border: the line that marks where one country ends and another begins.

continent: a large body of land separated from other bodies of land by an ocean or sea. There are seven continents in the world.

cube: a small square (noun); to cut into small squares (verb).

culture: a set of behaviors—including food, music, and clothing—that is typical of a group of people.

cumin: seeds that are ground into a powder and used to flavor foods.

cured: a process of preserving foods for later use. Olives are cured in salt or chemicals. They will not spoil for many years.

descendants: people in your family who are born after you, usually your children.

fast: the act of not eating anything or not eating certain foods, like meat. Fasting is usually done for religious reasons.

hard-boiled: eggs that are cooked in their shell so they are solid, not runny.

harvest: the time of year when foods are ripe and ready to be picked.

kebab: cubes of meat and vegetables that are cooked on a stick.

Mediterranean Sea: the body of water between Europe and Africa. It reaches from the coast of Spain to the coast of Israel.

Muhammad: the founder of the Middle Eastern religion called Islam. He was born in Mecca, Saudi Arabia, in the 6th century.

olive oil: oil used for cooking that is made from crushed olives.

pinch: the amount that you can pick up with your first finger and thumb.

pita bread: a flat bread with a pocket in the middle.

Qur'an: the book that holds all the laws and writings of Islam.

sacrifice: to give up something that you like very much.

simmer: to cook on a very low heat.

spices: ingredients that are used to add flavor to foods.

steep: to let ingredients stand in hot water so the flavors come out.

tattoo: markings on the skin that are sometimes permanent.

Bibliography

Blauer, Ettagale, and Jason Lauré. *Morocco.* New York: Children's Press, 1999.

Faruqi, Ismail al-, and Lamya al-Faruqi. *Cultural Atlas of Islam.* New York: Macmillan, 1986.

Hermes, Jules. *The Children of Morocco.* Minneapolis: Carolrhoda Books, 1995.

Hintz, Martin. *Morocco.* Chicago: Children's Press, 1985.

Morse, Kitty. *Cooking at the Kasbah: Recipes from My Moroccan Kitchen.* San Francisco: Chronicle Books, 1998.

Moslimany, Ann P. el-. *Zaki's Ramadan Fast.* Seattle: Amica Publishing House, 1994.

Seward, Pat. *Morocco.* New York: Marshall Cavendish, 1995.

Webb, Lois Sinaiko. *Holidays of the World Cookbook for Students.* Phoenix, Ariz.: Oryx Press, 1995.

websites:

http://www.holidayfestival.com

http://www.kittymorse.com

Index